PROMISE TEACHER

A classroom battles with their feelings and emotions to understand cancer's attack on their teacher

By

CYNTHIA LOCKE-HENDERSON, LICSW, LCSW-C, PH.D.

JayMedia
Publishing

ISBN: 978-1-7334432-6-5

I have tried to recreate events, locales and conversations from my memories of them. In order to maintain their anonymity in some instances I have changed the names of individuals and places. I may have changed some identifying characteristics and details such as physical properties, occupations and places of residence.

First printing, 2020.

JayMedia Publishing
Laurel, MD 20708

www.publishing.jaymediagroup.net

DEDICATION

This book is dedicated to a 5th grade teacher, Ms. Curbarb, who considered her students part of her family. When she learned of her cancer diagnosis, she shared it with her students. They expressed their fears of losing her and the pain each felt during her absences. They expressed their emotions in their words, behavior, art, and writing. These students responded to their teacher as if she held a space in their hearts similar to their mothers.

I thanked the students for allowing me to share their battle to understand that something bad was happening to a very good person. They allowed me, their social worker, to be their mediator, when others did not seem to understand the pain they felt after Ms. Curbarb's revelation to them.

This is their story and their attempt to hold on to her promise to them.

TABLE OF CONTENTS

FOREWORD

To God be the glory for the things He has done!
To God be the glory for the things He has done!

I first want to express my gratitude to God for trusting me to be an example for others who would face the dreaded announcement from a doctor, "You have cancer". It is said that the trials we go through in life are not for us, but to help others go through the same illness victoriously.

I thank God that because of my cancer, some of my students prayed to God for the first time in their lives, asking Him to heal me and not take me from them. I truly believe their sincere childlike faith had a lot to do with my healing.

It is my prayer that after going through their rebellion, anger, and refusal to be compliant, the students and I would learn a lesson of growth, and that it would be reaffirmed in their hearts that there is a God who hears and answers prayers.

I want the readers of this book to know that my students are also survivors. They have survived many different substitute teachers during my illness. The administration did not initially recognize that my students were grieving and angry because someone that they had trusted and had developed a loving relationship with, was no longer present in their daily lives.

The author of my story was our school social worker, Dr. Henderson. She was the lifeline for me and so many teachers, students, and families. She was always willing to help with behavioral issues and making sure that the students received the additional educational support they needed to be successful scholars.

Dr. Henderson made sure the students had proper clothing, eyeglasses, and plenty of love. She conducted lessons for the students on self-esteem, bullying, and how to recognize and report sexual abuse. She was present in my classroom when I discussed with my students my diagnosis of breast cancer, which was the beginning of their journey of grief and loss for me. Dr. Henderson was the lifeline that kept me and my students connected during my illness. She gave them opportunities to write letters, make cards, and would occasionally make phone calls for one of my students who cried almost every day.

Dr. Henderson arranged reading lessons over the phone so that I had the opportunity to hear each student read. Then I would ask them comprehension questions about what they had read.

She also made another phone call before their state test, so that I could encourage them to do well.

Dr. Henderson was instrumental in making sure their graduation was carried out just as if I had been there to plan it. I told my students that I would fight to be present at their graduation.

To my students, I still have your cards and letters and I will always remember your prayers.

To God be the glory for the things He has done!

Ms. Curbarb

PREFACE

This book was written by a school social worker who observed the grief process of students and staff members when a 5th grade teacher, Ms. Curbarb, articulated the words, *"I have Cancer."*

Dr. Cynthia Locke Henderson, the school social worker, looked for stories similar to the patterns of responses demonstrated by students, when their teacher shared her cancer diagnosis with them. There were many books about children's responses when their mom or a family member was diagnosed with cancer. Yet, these books did not address the uniqueness of these students.

Efforts were made to locate any books that spoke to the needs of this 5th grade class. Cancer organizations were contacted for resources, but did not have any resources that seemed to fit this class. After 26 years in a school setting, to Dr. Henderson, this situation seemed to have a unique set of experiences.

Dr. Henderson became the social worker/therapist for this teacher, the students, and the parents during this troubling time and decided this book had to be written. Interactions with Ms. Curbarb, from her initial disclosure of her cancer, and the frequent therapeutic sessions with students during the unfolding of this story, led to the development of this book.

This true story begins in an inner-city urban school with students representing all four quadrants of the city. There were many extraordinary students from diverse cultures. When you put them all together in this 5th grade class, each small unique piece was part of a bigger puzzle.

This puzzle emerges on a day when one can hear the phrase, "Trick or Treat". The trick was finding out if, after receiving such devastating news, this teacher would be able to continue effectively teaching her class. The treat was the revelation of circumstances exposed during this challenging time.

Ms. Curbarb made a promise to her students the day she revealed her diagnosis, "*I will fight with all of my might to come back to your graduation*". Read about the challenges here in this story.

The teacher and the students' names have been changed in this story to protect their privacy and confidentiality.

CHAPTER 1

PLANNING FOR DISCLOSURE

October 31, 2013. This Thursday, for teachers, was the day for the school-wide Fall Festival. For the students, it was a day for wearing a character's costume, eating treats and attending the fall dance. Ms. Curbarb told her students that she would not be in during the morning because she had a doctor's appointment. That did not matter to her students because they were focused on Fall Festival activities. The students were excited about the costume parade walk around the school with the hopes of winning the "Best Costume" prizes. Afterwards, all of the students would meet in the gym for the fall dance.

October 31, 2013 was a different day for Ms. Curbarb. Initially, she took a half day off for the doctor's appointment. Later, she requested a full day off when she received the results of her mammogram from her doctor. Ms. Curbarb shared her news with the head administrator and was granted the remainder of the day off.

The information from the doctor created a need for her to go home and pray to her Father, God. She approached her Father on bended knees with a request for strength to get through this trial.

Without her knowledge, the administrator had informed some staff members about her news. The report from her doctor was given to the whole staff at the end of the day during a brief meeting. This disclosure was devastating to the staff.

A melancholy mood overwhelmed the teachers as they began processing the news. Tears began to fall from the eyes of some teachers, while others were very silent as they signed out of school for the day. This was not how Ms. Curbarb wanted the staff to find out.

At home, Ms. Curbarb began to think about how she should tell her class. It was important to her that the news was not given to her students fragmentally. Knowing their histories and backgrounds caused her to give special consideration as to how she would inform them. She was a lady who often thought about the feelings of others before she thought about herself.

Her first reaction was to pray and absorb the report given by her doctor. Normally, when a doctor calls you back to go over a mammogram, you immediately think, *Cancer.* You ask yourself, *Is it benign or malignant?* Ms. Curbarb's prayer on the way to the doctor was, "Father, thy will be done!" She reached a resolve and immediately concluded that this battle was not hers. It was the Lord's. She thought, *I will pray first and begin praising God as He takes me through this test.*

When Ms. Curbarb came to school on the next day, she became aware that news of her illness had been shared with the staff. Some teachers approached her with tears in their eyes and sad expressions. She told them she would be all right.

As they approached the elevator to go to class, she told them, "If you feel like you need to come to me crying, DON'T! Your sadness is a distraction to my faith that God will heal me. The best thing you can do for me is pray."

In her mind she thought, *I will be glad when this elevator reaches the third floor. I don't want to join these friends with tears and sadness. I don't want to go into my classroom crying.*

She continued on to her classroom of 5th grade students. Ms. Curbarb mentally rehearsed what she needed to say and how to say it. She considered the impact her news would have on some of her students who had existing personal crises and situations at school, home and in the community. She considered the students who were dealing with relation-ship issues within the school and class. In addition, she considered all of those who called her "Momma", and saw her as their second mother. She continued to pray and ask God to give her the words to say.

She decided that honesty was the best way to inform her students. They had been honest with her when they were going through difficult times at home, in school and in the community. Children have a talent that allows them to feel genuine honesty and care. Children have been taught to be honest since preschool when they listened to stories such as "Pinocchio." Of course, Ms. Curbarb did not want her proverbial nose to grow as she disclosed her condition to her students. She decided to tell the full truth about her diagnosis and treatment plans.

Ms. Curbarb and Dr. Ms. L., the school social worker, began devel-oping an action plan for telling students about her diagnosis on Friday, November 1, 2013.

She wanted the day to begin with the usual lessons. It was important that she give them some strategies to use for the upcoming standardized test. Success on standardized testing was extremely important for her 5th graders. Their performance on standardized tests impacted their accep-tance to desired middle schools.

It was also important to Ms. Curbarb that her students did not hear about her condition randomly from others. Equally important to her was that her students had time to ask questions.

She decided that she and her students would talk in their classroom at the end of the day during the designated meeting time and would have additional support staff in attendance, along with Dr. Ms. L.

Typically, on Mondays in Ms. Curbarb's math class, she would began with a review lesson from the previous week, and then introduce a new math concept.

At home that past weekend, this class had celebrated "Halloween", and like most children they had a weekend filled with candy and Halloween parties. The students' sugar levels were almost lethal, as indicated by their hyperactive behaviors and "bouncing off the wall" syndrome during class. First Ms. Curbarb politely said, "settle down" so that class could begin. Normally, if students did not respond to that, she would have simply ignored the noise and would have begun writing classwork on the smart board. When those strategies did not work, she would simply look at students and not say a word. Surprisingly, that last strategy worked the best.

Each fall, teachers and students spent a lot of time getting ready for testing. Students were tired of rehearsing for testing. They hated studying for and taking tests.

Ms. Curbarb made sure she taught little strategies to help students remember information needed for the tests. She created games to help students learn. She even offered to purchase a sub sandwich of their choice for lunch, when they did well within their ability. Her goal was for every student to learn math in such a way that it could be remembered for tests, classwork assignments, homework assignments and everyday activities.

Some sample test activities were as follows:

1. Sharon bakes 10 cookies. She puts 7 M & M chips on each cookie. Draw a tape diagram and label the total amounts of M & M chips as C.

7									

    C
    $10 \times 7 = C$
    $C = 70$

2. Mr. James arranges 48 dry-erase markers into 8 equal groups for his math station. Draw a tape diagram and label the number of markers in each group as V. Write an equation and solve for V.

V							

$$48$$
$$48 - 8 = v$$

$$(40 \div 8) \ (8 \div 8)$$
$$5 \times 1 = 5$$

Class began with the usual learning distractions. Sometimes students would purposely get in trouble or request a bathroom break when they did not want to do the work. This was no problem for Ms. Curbarb on this particular Friday because she was determined that students would get the strategies that she had planned for them. Little did they know that Ms. Curbarb was trying to teach all that she could because she would not be there for the Partnership for Assessment of Readiness for College and Careers (PARCC) test.

If they needed extra help, she gave them a choice to stay in during recess or come back in the evening. She contacted the parents if she felt a student needed help at home. She gave parents web sites that referred to the lessons that were taught during the school day.

Ms. Curbarb believed that she should never give up on a child who wanted to learn, or on the children who had other issues blocking them from learning.

In Ms. Curbarb's experience, the number of students that loved math and the number of students that did not love math, was vastly different. However, she would turn lessons into competitions between groups or she would give points to those students that could come to the board and solve the math problems. This would often equalize the playing field. On this Monday after Halloween, Ms. Curbarb taught her class with a little extra passion.

The "meeting time" to share the diagnosis with her students was quickly approaching. She knew that her students would be affected by the news about her cancer. She planned to allow time to answer every question that the students asked.

She also wanted students to remember the steps to solve most of their math problems. She said to her students, "I want you to know how to do these problems anytime, anywhere with or without me". Little did the students know the prophecy given with that statement.

Throughout the day, she kept reflecting on the time that was coming when she would be at home receiving treatment and not in the classroom teaching her students. This greatly concerned her and she wanted her students to be prepared for their upcoming test.

Solving word problems was significantly more difficult for many students who had reading difficulties. So, Ms. Curbarb used acronyms to help her students learn and remember. She taught her students about using the RACE concept to answer open-ended questions. Although the RACE acronym did not mean get in a car to participate in a race, she taught students to think about racing a car to the finish line. Their answers were not complete until they incorporated each letter of the RACE concept.

Ms. Curbarb said, "You can't reach the finish line if you stop half way."

RESTATE the question.

ANSWER the question that is being asked.

CITE evidence from the text.

EXPLAIN your answer. Use multiple sentences.

When students did not understand how to solve their math problems, Ms. Curbarb invited them to come to the "big table" where she would work with them one-on-one and in small groups. There were students whom she knew needed her support daily.

That Friday, the math lesson was no different from any other Friday. She taught math with passion all of the time. At the end of the lesson, Ms. Curbarb called out, "Asia, come to the big table so I can make sure you understand the 'RACE' concept."

There were some students that Ms. Curbarb always made sure she called to the big table or she would go to their desks, and even give them a few minutes after class. Ms. Curbarb had a way of pulling kids for help without embarrassing them.

Students knew Asia had a lot going on at home and needed the extra love and help. Some of them wanted to have a reason to get special attention like

Asia. Sometimes they picked at her, but most of the time they understood her. Asia did not smile a lot and most times appeared shy and sad. Asia had a beautiful smile, if you could get her to smile. Asia looked like a different girl when she understood the math. She smiled when she was in her therapy session working towards managing her feelings about her home situation. She smiled when positive efforts about her mom were discussed. It was in therapy where she interacted most. It was there in the play therapy corner where she could create the kind of home that she wanted.

Other times, Ms. Curbarb allowed students peer support. Some students would remain at the end of the day if their parents gave permission. Ms. Curbarb faithfully prayed during her morning and free time for her students before they entered the class. Some students would slip up to the room during Ms. Curbarb's free time.

Students frequently misbehaved when they did not feel like learning; however, they could always count on Ms. Curbarb's support whenever they got serious about learning. Almost every student's parent's number was in Ms. Curbarb's phone. She cared enough to include their parents, if she felt it would motivate the students.

For some of her students, Ms. Curbarb was like a second mother. The way she would look at you, or when she sat down and said nothing, were indicators that students needed to "get it together". That often worked without a telephone call to parents, grandparents, aunts and sometimes dad. When all else failed she referred some students to Dr. Ms. L.

Ms. Curbarb started class by putting a problem on the board that made students wonder "Where do I begin solving it?"

$$2 \times 4^2 + 5^2 + (26 - 1)$$

She told them to use the "PEMDAS" rule.

"PEMDAS?" Allen asked, barely pronouncing the word.

He was so lost. Ms. Curbarb had mercy on him and taught him and the class how to say the word and then the order that each letter represented. She knew Allen was not the only student who could not pronounce the word. She told them another way to remember PEMDAS is to remember the phrase: **P**lease **E**xcuse **M**y **D**ear **A**unt **S**ally.

After putting this problem on the board, she directed students to follow the steps to the PEMDAS rule.

Many students responded with complaints. Yoruba spoke out and said, "That's hard, we can't do that problem.

He wanted to have a basic problem with one operation. Ms. Curbarb directed him and others to stop complaining and to simply solve it one step at a time following the rule PEMDAS.

Of course, just like "Mr. Gibbs" on the TV show *NCIS of Los Angeles*, Ms. Curbarb had a "rule" for everything. She would say, "Let's say it out loud so that your brains can hear it, 'PEMDAS."

P   Parentheses first

E   Exponents (i.e. Powers and Square Roots, etc.)

M   Multiplication and

D   Division (left-to-right)

A   Addition and

S   Subtraction (left-to-right)

Ms. Curbarb had a way of always making a difficult math problem easy. Students walked with her through the example as they were working on PEMDAS stepping-stones.

$$2 \times 4^2 + 52 : (26 - 1) = 2 \times 4^2 + 5^2 : (26 - 1)$$
$$= 2 \times 4^2 + 5^2 : (25)$$
$$= 2 \times 4^2 + 5^2 : 25$$
$$= 2 \times 16 + 1$$
$$= 32 + 1$$
$$= 33$$

There were some students that understood quicker than others. Chuck was one of those students. He understood everything. The nice thing about him was that he would help anyone. He was a big kid with a big heart, yet he did not use his size to bully others.

In fact, if there was a fight, he would try to stop it or get help.

She gave the students problems that would definitely be on the ANet

(Achievement Network) test and the PARCC test.

The students in the class were of various academic levels and social emotional needs. They were students that required extensive academic support and were referred to Special Education for support when general education interventions had failed.

Once identified for Special Education, these students had difficulty in class, because other students would tease them for being in Special Education. As school social worker, Dr. Ms. L also provided these students with related services and an alternative location when the teasing became unmanageable. Collaboration among the special educator, the teacher and the social worker, began with a plan where the special educator came to the classroom to identify the students' needs. These needs would be addressed in the special educator's classroom. As these students showed improvement and improved management of their behaviors and emotions, the teasing decreased.

Ms. Curbarb was very skillful at making sure the students were not embarrassed and were given special positive attention when they were successful. No wonder her students loved her. The students in her classroom had lots of personal issues which included foster care placement, adoption issues, parental neglect, cultural adjustment, blended family issues, fatherless homes, poor parent relationships and unresolved grief issues.

They would frequently share their issues with each other and with Ms. Curbarb. These issues added to the difficulty they had in math, and contributed to frequent behavior problems in the classroom, in the lunchroom, on the playground, and in the community.

Ms. Curbarb managed to love them in such a unique way that they all felt they were special to her. Students loved that lady and looked forward to seeing her every week. They were a family. Overall, daily attendance was pretty good. There were late arrivals for a few students; sometimes the tardiness was within the student's control, and sometimes it was not.

Ms. Curbarb had to consider all of these variables for her class when planning to tell them about her cancer. Since her cancer diagnosis was advanced, there was a limited amount time for her to tell her students. The first week of January 2014 was going to be her last week of school before surgery and treatment.

Ms. Curbarb and Dr. Ms. L discussed anticipated responses based on the individual dynamics of each student. They concluded that the end of the first week of January, during the last period of the school day would be the time to talk with students. They both wanted to give students a time to ask questions and process the information about her illness. Dr. Ms. L decided that students needed to leave that day with a level of hope.

Ms. Curbarb chose music that was common and encouraging to the students. This music played softly in the background and was sung by the students at the end of the session. The butterfly was used as a symbol of hope for the students, because it goes through stages that were not so pretty. At the end of the stages, butterflies come out with so many diversities of beauty. Blank cards were decorated with butterflies given to the students to write encouraging messages for Ms. Curbarb to read during her treatment. Both Dr. Ms. L and Ms. Curbarb made plans to remain after the dismissal bell or as long as needed for the students.

Dr. Ms. L always tried to end her group's session with a sense of hopefulness and with a task that connected to the next session. This disclosure session was going to be slightly different. These students would not be seeing Ms. Curbarb for several weeks once she had surgery and began treatment. Chances were her absence might extend up to or past the class graduation date.

Dr. Ms. L's task for these students was to be able to shift their focus away from the sad news they were about to hear, to a reasonable level of hope. In exchange, students would focus on helping their teacher by designing and writing individual cards of encouragement, to accompany her through cancer treatment. All of the students would want their usual hug, normally given as they exited the classroom each evening. Dr. Ms. L hesitated because of Ms. Curbarb's diagnosis of breast cancer. Noticing the hesitation, Ms. Curbarb said that hugging her would not cause her discomfort, therefore, the hugging/touching moments were included in the plans for her last day. Dr. Ms. L would also make herself available the following week when students would return to school without the presence of Ms. Curbarb. Given the closeness of Ms. Curbarb and her students, Dr. Ms. L planned to have a flexible schedule that would allow her to be available for the students. She also planned time with Ms. Curbarb at home, in the hospital, and post-surgery.

CHAPTER 2

ALL MY CHILDREN

Some of the planning for sharing the cancer diagnosis with the students was changed when Dr. Ms. L. was called to assist with an emergency meeting involving an irritated parent and the principal. The end of the school day was nearing, and Ms. Curbarb wanted to tell her students so that they would have the weekend with family and friends to adjust to the news. She planned to have Dr. Ms. L. with her at the beginning of the session, but that plan seemed to fade with time. Ms. Curbarb thought it was important to have all the necessary people available when revealing such traumatic news to her class, but time did not seem to be on her side.

Ms. Curbarb's dilemma was that she was providing traumatic information to her students, in addition to the social and emotional concerns that they already had. She wanted Dr. Ms. L to be present. There were 19 students in her class and each one had their own traumatic experiences.

Their individual stories were shared with her at different times either by them or their parents. Ms. Curbarb had most of the cell phone and home phone numbers of parents saved into the contacts on her phone. Their parents also had her cell phone number and could call whenever they needed to talk to her. At "warp speed", Ms. Curbarb, while reflecting on several situations her students were dealing with, decided to proceed with the help of their gym teacher - someone that each student was familiar with.

Allen. Allen's family was from Africa. Allen wrote his feelings about the people that were important in his life in a book. One of them was his grandfather who had been in the hospital and then in hospice. He talked about going to his room many evenings after school because of the uncontrollable flow of tears after the eventual death of his grandfather. Allen's mom would often talk with Ms. Curbarb and the school social worker, Dr. Ms. L about Allen's sadness. Writing in his book during his sessions with the social worker seemed to lessen Allen's sadness.

Sandra. Sandra was a very bright student who often missed many days in school because of a rare condition. Ms. Curbarb would make sure she had schoolwork at home to compensate for lost time at school. Sandra said it was hard for her to make friends because she was sick so often. She missed her classmates and had difficulty building relationships. Sometimes, Sandra's friends were annoyed with her frequent need for attention. She loved Ms. Curbarb because she always seemed to understand and take time with her.

Tirana. Tirana was the last of four siblings who had gone through Eagleville Elementary School. Ms. Curbarb had been there for Tirana's older siblings and her mom had gone through many challenges during her time in Ms. Curbarb's class.

Tirana had a distracted and short attention span like her mom. Sometimes it was difficult for her, when she was stressed and tried to do her best for her mom. She carried some of her mom's emotional struggles. At this point in her life, Tirana's mom had stability, took care of Tirana and made sure that she had the best of everything. She was changing from the distracted person she had been in Ms. Curbarb's class. Others could see Tirana's mom's progress and praised her for her change.

Tirana's mom landed a job at Eagleville Elementary School and was loved by staff. For Tirana, though, it was challenging to have her mom working in her school, being friends with her teachers, and on her case if she did anything that was inappropriate.

Sasha. Sasha lived with her dad and his friend in a small apartment which included five children and two adults. Sasha's living situation was known by her classmates.

One of Sasha's teachers had also taught Sasha's mother. Sasha was frequently in contact with her mother and efforts were being made for her to join her mom. The crowded living situation and time lost from school because of the transitions between her parents, impacted Sasha's mood. Sasha's mom's promise to find a better living situation for her and her sisters was not coming fast enough.

Asia. Asia lived with a mom who had difficulty providing for her and her brothers. Out of the four children that her mom had, Asia struggled the most academically and socially. She had difficulty building relationships because she did not have candy and snacks to share. Other times she would get teased about her uniform not being neat or about her hair. She felt intimidated but tolerated the teasing most of the time. Yet, there were times when she would become angry and lash out verbally or physically at others. Ms. Curbarb and Dr. Ms. L. were almost always able to work with Asia one-on-one or send her to the counseling suite to complete her work.

After gathering documentation, Asia was evaluated for support from Special Education. Asia worked well in Special Education but she had difficulty with transitioning from one class to the next. Her classmates from Ms. Curbarb's room figured that she had gone to a Special Education class and chose to tease her about it. Once in the Special Educator's class, Asia enjoyed working with students that had academic difficulties similar to hers. Ms. Curbarb and her Special Educator always encouraged her as she demonstrated progress and was motivated to learn more.

Ms. Curbarb's class was like a puzzle with many pieces. Some big, some little, some shaped awkwardly, some pieces that seemed not to belong and some pieces that required a lot of negotiation to make them fit, but Ms. Curbarb had the skills, strategies, and compassion to see the puzzle completed by the end of each school year. Each new student entered her classroom with many stories, invited her into their stories, got angry with her, yet surrendered to learning from her, and finally loved her and left for their next school experience saturated with the love.

Kesha. Kesha was a student who needed to be loved but was not willing to let anyone know that she needed it. She was a very independent and intelligent person. Kesha focused on doing well academically, so that she did not have to ask for help. She only related to some students and had a few friends in Ms. Curbarb's class. With a younger sibling attending the same school, Kesha was responsible for getting her sibling to and from school. This was not a favorite thing for her to do. She did not seem to want that responsibility. Occasionally her grandparent would bring her younger sibling. Her mom worked most of the time and needed Kesha's help with getting her sibling to school. That responsibility created friction between Kesha and her mom. It was evident by some of their interactions during school visits that Kesha had some difficulty getting along with her. Kesha frequently came to school angry. On a few occasions she got into fights with peers. She frequently got into confrontations with some of her teachers. Sometimes she began her day in an angry mood, and would isolate herself in the classroom, during recess and lunch time. If anyone stepped near her perimeter of anger, a fight or argument usually broke out. She would fight a boy as quick as she would fight a girl. Ms. Curbarb used to call Kesha's mother whenever there were behavior problems at school, until she became aware of the hostility between the two. Eventually, Kesha was referred to Dr. Ms. L. for counseling and she met with Kesha's mom and Ms. Curbarb. Since Kesha's academic performance was excellent, Dr. Ms. L. began the session focusing on Kesha's positive behaviors. Kesha was a quick learner and demonstrated academic strength. The three of them would intermittently talk about her angry moods. Her mom provided an explanation for Kesha's anger and gave some clarity to her problems. Dr. Ms. L referred Kesha to Peer Mediation. Mediation with specific peer mediators was helpful sometimes. Kesha preferred to keep her problems private most of the time.

Eddie. Eddie was a child that expressed his frustration with tearful outbursts of emotions that resulted in him walking out of the class, getting into fights, disrupting the class or getting sent to the school social worker. When Eddie was having a good day, he was on task, raised his hand and participated well in class. Eddie could build relationships with anyone, but he had difficulty keeping them. When students created rumors about him or he thought they had said something about him, Eddie would immediately begin crying or becoming aggressive towards his peers.

Eddie was very caring and concerned about Ms. Curbarb whenever she was absent for more than a day. There was a period when Ms. Curbarb was absent from school to have a procedure done, Eddie had difficulty with the substitute. The next day Eddie saw Ms. Curbarb get out of the car to enter the school. He jumped out of his mom's moving car to run and give Ms. Curbarb a hug. It was a dangerous thing to do, but Eddie survived. Ms. Curbarb warned him of the danger. Ms. Curbarb's attendance was very good even on days when she did not feel her best. She seemed to get a burst of energy when she assumed her role as teacher for all of her "children".

Other pieces to the puzzle that made up Ms. Curbarb's class included students like Yoruba, whose family was from one of the islands in the Caribbean Sea. Yoruba's dad was very involved with his schooling.in addition, he attended every parent meeting or conference. He would always respond to Ms. Curbarb when she would call to solicit his support with making sure Yoruba was finishing major projects, like Science Projects. Yoruba avoided getting into behavior difficulties in school, partially because his father was a frequent visitor there. Yoruba had been raised to take education seriously. He had a brother that had major physical disabilities. When his little brother entered school, he required medical accommodations to keep him in school in a less restricted environment. Yoruba's father made sure he did not feel a lack of attention because of his younger brother. He looked out for his little brother and helped as needed.

Paul was another student who did not cause nor engage in behaviors that negatively impacted his learning process. Paul was caring and not self-centered. He was smart and did not mind helping other students who needed help with assignments. Similar to some other students in his class, he had the responsibility of getting his little brother to class in the morning, and watching him at the end of the school day, until his dad came home. Dad did not always arrive at school by dismissal; therefore, Paul would find activities to participate in or simply go to a classroom where teachers were staying later into the evening. Paul's family's living situation varied. Due to illnesses, attendance was a concern for his little brother. Paul was very focused on being successful in school and no longer being homeless. He had hopes of going to the college of his choice and someday making life better for his mother, little brother and himself.

Steven was the total opposite of Paul. He was adopted and seemed to be cherished by his adopted mother. Steven often did things that seemed to be attention seeking behaviors. When his friends would not accept him in their group, he would say he was going to kill himself. Other times he would become so overwhelmed with anger to the point that his mom had to be called. Steven was often gifted with exceptional fashions and technology. He would become braggadocios around his peers who simply ignored him. Steven would then go into self-pity mode. Ms. Curbarb frequently had conferences with his mom to seek help with managing Steven's behavior. Steven participated in a male empowerment group. His selection into the group made him feel that he was better than those that did not get selected. Dr. Ms. L. frequently met with Steven when he was in crisis and during the male empowerment group. She attempted to get Steven to realize that he was chosen. When students are adopted, they are invited into families that made the choice to love a child that was not born into their families. Dr. Ms. L. created opportunities for Steven to be in leadership positions. Other times she would work with Steven to recognize others as they assumed leadership roles. Steven's adopted mom invested time and money to make Steven feel loved. She also solicited outside support from family and friends. Steven showed some improvement when he served as a peer mediator. Functioning as a peer mediator made him value the time and attention given to him by his adopted mother. Ms. Curbarb would make Steven feel loved by awarding his academic strengths and behavior management with a special lunch or other incentives. Dr. Ms. L. would allow Steven to earn a chance for social enrichment field trips.

Ms. Curbarb carried her students in her heart and in her daily prayers. As time grew near to tell her students about her illness, their emotional differences were included in her plans. They were different but they were all her "children". It was important that she disclosed her illness to her students. She did not want them to get the news of her illness in fragmented pieces. Her class had enough pieces to their life puzzles without her adding to them. They were her children and she had to tell them. She knew that they would worry once she left for treatment. She had always been honest and straight forward with them. This was not the time to keep her diagnosis from them.

Teachers are a necessary part of life

A teacher takes the position as my mom and caregiver away from home. She or he is the lady or gentleman that dresses up Monday through Friday just for me. She or he loves like my mom or my dad. They push me to be my best, pass their test, then they scold me when I cheat myself from being the best that I can be.

Dr. Cynthia Locke Henderson

Teachers understand my difficulties at home and make me forget all about it as they teach me to feel love during school hours. They can't always change my personal situations, but they help me focus on the individual things that I can change about me.

Dr. Cynthia Locke Henderson

Teachers are moms and dads away from home.
Teachers are friends that want to have a part in my maturity and growth.
Teachers etch their emotional imprints of love that are remembered long after I am away from them.

Dr. Cynthia Locke Henderson

School Social Workers are The Connection Factor
Students, Teachers, Parents and The Community

School social workers are similar to a paperclip that holds everyone and everything together as participants make sense of the chaos.

Dr. Cynthia Locke Henderson

School social workers meet everyone where they are and invite them to a joint production beneficial to all.

Dr. Cynthia Locke Henderson

A school social worker occupies two seats at the table of decisions, one seat as the advocate to ensure that students are treated fairly, and the other seat to be the student's voice no matter what that voice is saying.

Dr. Cynthia Locke Henderson

CHAPTER 3

I HAVE CANCER

School staff was informed of Ms. Curbarb's diagnosis at a staff meeting. Some could not believe it and came to her directly to confirm her diagnosis. The common feeling of the staff was, *What do we do next?* After the staff meeting, Ms. Curbarb shared the elevator up to the third floor with some of her colleagues. They were sad and silent; some were about to cry. Ms. Curbarb did not want to be overwhelmed so she told them, "I will be alright. If you feel like you need to come to me crying, DON'T! Your sadness is a distraction to my faith that God will heal me. The best thing you can do for me is pray."

The staff was aware that Ms. Curbarb was a praying lady. This fight against cancer was just another challenge of her faith and the grace of God would equip her with what she needed to get through. The staff respected her wishes to hold their tears for their personal crying moments. Some came to her after they had their crying moments. Some came just for a hug and to let her know that they would be praying for her. A long-time staff member and friend said to her, "Why you?" Ms. Curbarb responded, "Why not me? I am just a person like anyone. This is the challenge that had my name on it."

Some staff said that they would be praying for Ms. Curbarb's strength. Ms. Curbarb said, "Don't pray for my strength, pray for grace. Grace is God's unmerited favor. With God's favor, everything I need is under his grace." Forbearance/long suffering is one of the fruits of the Spirit under God's grace. Galatians 5:22-23 (KJV) says, "But the fruit of the Spirit is love, joy, peace, longsuffering, gentleness, goodness, faith, meekness, temperance: against such there is no law." Ms. Curbarb thought to herself, *If I have the fruits, I will get through this challenge also.*

The scheduled time for Ms. Curbarb and Dr. Ms. L. to talk with the students was rapidly approaching. Dr. Ms. L was called to the office three times to resolve student and parent conflicts. Time did not seem to be on their side. Since Dr. Ms. L. was still in the meeting with the principal and a parent,

Ms. Curbarb decided to proceed without her for fear the dismissal bell would ring before she had a chance to share her diagnosis with the students. It was the end of the day and the gym teacher and a support teacher were present. The students were unusually quiet during the end of this school day. Although Ms. Curbarb had given the students basic strategies that would get them through the upcoming testing, telling them that she had cancer was not as easy as telling them they were going to take another test. This was different. Ms. Curbarb thought the impact of what she was going to tell her students was one of the hardest things she ever had to consider. How could she make it easy for them? She and her students were like a family. This news would be devastating for them.

On January 3, 2014, Ms. Curbarb stood before her students and said, "I know you all have been aware of me coming in late or leaving early for doctor appointments. The doctors were conducting tests to determine if I had cancer. The answer is yes, I do have cancer." Immediately after she told the students, tears began to flow uncontrollably down several faces. Some students simply put their heads on the desk, while others seemed shocked and in disbelief. One or two of them stepped out to the restroom, while others just looked and wanted to hug her, not knowing if it would hurt. They simply wanted to be hugged by their teacher and second mom. Ms.

Curbarb could feel their desire. She approached some of the students and gave a comforting touch or hug to let them know it was okay to touch her.

Chuck, a very smart and considerate student, cried and said, "I lost my uncle and now I am going to lose my teacher." Ms. Curbarb said with assurance, "I did not say I was going to die. I am going to fight it with all my might." She also told them that she would fight to be at their graduation. Ms. Curbarb did as she often had to do and gave her students hope during a time of disclosing challenging news. These were her "children" and she cared about their emotional state after getting such traumatic news. Chuck had a single mom. His uncle was his strong male figure. It was clear that Chuck had not resolved grief issues surrounding the death of his uncle. Chuck took a lot of ridicule because of his size. Despite his size, he was a very respectful and intelligent young man. He frequently walked away, ignored ridicule, and maintained the position as one of the smartest students in her class. The news of his teacher having cancer was something he could not walk away from. He did not care about the ridicule; he broke down and cried along with everyone else in the class. David, a Muslim student said, "Let's pray." Amidst tears, some of the other students said, "I don't know how to pray, I never prayed before."

Both Ms. Curbarb and the gym teacher said, "Prayer is nothing but talking to God, telling Him what you desire, or asking for something from Him." The students and the teachers joined hands and formed a circle. Each prayed with the theme of Ms. Curbarb getting better and coming back to them. The students responded in accordance with Dr. Elizabeth Kubler-Ross' first state of grief. They responded with shock and disbelief that this could not be happening to a lady like Ms. Curbarb. None of them ever imagined that Ms. Curbarb, who came to school daily, could be found praying or humming a praise, and greeting each one of them with a smile in the morning whether she is feeling good or not, could have CANCER. No one could imagine that their day and week would end with the news they had just received. Limited words were said as tears flowed spontaneously in the group.

Dr. Ms. L. joined the group as they finished praying. The hurt from the news that they had just received was obvious by their sad faces and crying. The tears continued to flow as boxes of tissue made their way around the circle. The sadness and flowing of tears seemed unstoppable and overwhelming.

Prior to informing the students about the diagnosis of cancer, Dr. Ms. L. and Ms. Curbarb decided to work towards ending the time with students on an upbeat note and with hope. Ms. Curbarb requested that they continue to keep her in their prayers as she went through treatment. She also invited them to come to visit her once she notified them of a good time to come.

Dr. Ms. L. had prepared and distributed blank cards that she put butterflies on, along with statements that indicated they would be on their best behavior for Ms. Curbarb. Dr, Ms. L. said to them, that's similar to how the butterfly goes through a difficult metamorphosis to become a beautiful butterfly, they too would "fly". They encouraged Ms. Curbarb to get better and return to them. Students were asked to shift their focus to praying for Ms. Curbarb to get well so she could keep her promise (*"Fight with all her might to come back to them and be at their graduation"*). They were asked to write messages of encouragement for Ms. Curbarb to read during her recovery. Motivational music was played to transition the students to feelings of hope. The tears slowly stopped. Boys and girls began to write. Smiles of admiration replaced the tears and sadness. It was as if they would only think about her return. These were students who in the past had difficulty whenever they were asked to write an assignment. They began writing from their hearts. They wrote short messages, long messages, and some drew pictures. Since they would not be at her home to read them to her, they seemed to write their cards in a way that would speak directly to her. Before the song finished the first verse, students began to sing along with the music. Their tears dried up as they hugged each other and hugged Ms. Curbarb. They did not seem to feel that she was fragile. They seemed to see her as their second momma who was going away for a long time, and may not return. A part of them where hopeful that she would return. All they knew was that they wanted to feel her encouraging arms one more time before they were promoted to middle school. Students held on to her for a few moments as if thinking subconsciously that it might be their last hug. They hugged her as if their hugs were like memory foam that would stay in place to represent their individual hugs. They seemed to believe, with the benefit of hoping, that the hug would get them through the days ahead. Ms. Curbarb's last words as they left to go to their homes were, "Students please fly. Do well on the upcoming test. *I will see you at graduation.*" She promised to do all that she could do to come back. She encouraged them to believe in the prayers that they prayed.

Staff members came by to get a hug before she left. Ms. Curbarb's hugs had special powers. They respected her wishes earlier when she asked them to cry in their secret places and not to her. Ms. Curbarb asked that they come to her with hope and faith because that is what would get her through this. Some staff members tried very hard, but seemed unable to control their tears. Ms. Curbarb just hugged them and asked them to pray for her often. A few parents that normally picked up their children came by and gave her words of encouragement and she gave back words of encouragement.

Ms. Curbarb had a few moments of reflection in the room that was now void of children, void of noise, void of her student's responses to cancer, void of her efforts to teach, void of life but filled with prayer. Similar to the students praying for her, she left a prayer in room 302 to cover her students until her return. Walking out of that door that evening was like walking into a battle that only God would get her through. God's grace and her faith were the only things to get her through this new challenge. It was in this same room that she taught while struggling to help her husband fight his battle with a terminal illness. She thought to herself, *This time I am coming to you God, for me. I need to return to this room, these children and my son. God grant me the grace to do so.*

Where did this cancer come from? What did I need to learn in this test? I trust you God to keep my students until I return. Despite my current state of being, Lord I worship you because of who you are. This is a challenging trip on my way to your promise for me. I refuse to give up because of circumstances. I choose to trust you to help me keep my promise.

CHAPTER 4

THE WAITING GAME

Ms. Curbarb was under the doctor's care and had a few more months before she would have surgery on January 10, 2014. It was her desire to be able to work up to the date of her surgery. Students came to school more regular, perhaps to make sure they would see her or to make sure she did not die. Several students in her class seemed to feel that she had been given a death sentence when she announced that she had cancer. Chuck's initial response was, "You're going to die!" He was the only one to verbalize what several of them were thinking. Other students expressed their fears and anxiety of losing her by acting out in distracting ways such as: arguing with others, walking out of the classroom, not doing or completing work, etc.

Learning continued with some good days and some bad days. Ms. Curbarb seemed to have a grasp of her student's academic performances, social-emotional concerns, and their home dynamics. She avoided being overwhelmed by the student's emotional needs and behaviors by inviting them to come to the "Big Table" in groups or individually. Their time at the table was a time for them to have the teacher all to themselves. Looking back, it seemed that some students pretended not to understand in order to increase their time with Ms. Curbarb at the big table.

Sometimes it meant getting their parent on the telephone for added support with getting them in a learning mode.

Since some of the students from Ms. Curbarb's class were peer mediators, Dr. Ms. L. would activate them when needed. They had some insight into the troubling behaviors in class and school. At times, the same group of students had the same problems repeatedly. After repeated sessions, a peer mediator once said to the reoccurring group, "Grow Up". Believe it or not, that stopped the repeated need for mediation for some. This was somewhat a confrontational stance. This was not a technique that worked with all students. Dr. Ms. L discussed this with the mediators during wrap up and training sessions.

Ms. Curbarb had multiple strategies that she used. However, she remained aware that her students were responding to the impact of her news about cancer. She was fully aware of the impact her disclosure had on her students, the impact of their home situations, the impact of how their class was viewed by others in the school, and the impact of their limited and sometimes lack of effective social emotional functioning. She often grouped students according to their academic needs and how they interacted with others. Grouping was not etched in stone; flexibility was required as student's needs fluctuated. Ms. Curbarb and Dr. Ms. L were co-workers and friends. They frequently collaborated on how best to support her students. Collaboration occurred over lunch, when they drove home together, and during the weekly calls to each other. These students were in grief mode.

Asia was having difficulty before Ms. Curbarb's disclosure; however, her anxiety increased afterwards. Telephone calls to her caregivers and extended family helped Ms. Curbarb better understand her struggle. She missed her mom and was feeling that she would lose her teacher. She was grieving. Ms. Curbarb represented her school mom. Ms. Curbarb did not look down on her because she was not as well-groomed as others. When she did not have school supplies, Dr. Ms. L collaborated with Ms. Curbarb and made sure Asia had all the supplies needed. Asia was given a new backpack with all new items in it. Also, Ms. Speed, the school psychologist spent private time with Asia and was able to identify some of her academic deficits. Asia received support from the Special Educator who took her to her room which had several items that made learning fun and easier for Asia. Sometimes Ms. Speed came into the classroom to work with Asia. Before Ms. Curbarb left, she and Dr. Ms. L made sure Asia's graduation and educational plans were activated, and that she had everything she needed, including her white dress for graduation. There was a limited amount of time left before her departure for surgery; however, Ms. Curbarb was planning ahead.

Sammy was another student who did not live with his father. Sammy had good academic skills and was a quick learner. He struggled with self-esteem issues despite being a handsome guy. He struggled with other boys disliking him because he seemed to attract the attention of girls mostly. Ms. Curbarb used many strategies in the classroom to allow Sammy leadership opportunities. She allowed him to work with students that did not understand math and with students who were receptive to help. Chuck was another one of the students who was smart with low self-esteem. Ms. Curbarb matched the two fifth graders in such a way that they supported each other and both began developing good self-esteem. Their positions as peer mediators with Dr. Ms. L also added to improving their self-esteem. These two boys were among the top achievers in Ms. Curbarb's class.

Chuck and Sammy both had fathers that were not involved in their lives. Sammy had a few incidents when he could not manage the scrutiny of peers. There were some physical and verbal altercations. Ms. Curbarb referred Sammy for counseling with Dr. Ms. L. Like a mom, she figured the anger had a deeper source than what she saw in class and at school. During counseling, Sammy began writing his book about missing his father. Sammy looked on the web for images to include in his book. He pulled up a figure and said, "This is my dad." His picture was on a site that showed incarcerated individuals. As Sammy felt safe enough to share, he expressed very sad feelings about the absence of his father during counseling. He completed a therapeutic book project but did not share it with anyone except Ms. Curbarb. Sammy seemed to be a different student once he shared the story about his father during counseling. Dr. Ms. L. encouraged Sammy as he completed his therapy book. She told him that he can close it up and put it away. He could visit it any time he wanted to. He was in control of those feelings regarding his father.

Another interesting case in Ms. Curbarb's class was Sasha, one of five girls born to her mom. Sasha lived with her father and his friend. They lacked several resources needed for Ms. Curbarb's class. It did not take long for her to connect with Ms. Curbarb and she shared some of her challenges with her teacher. Ms. Curbarb and Dr. Ms. L. collaborated and got resources including uniforms for Sasha and her sisters. Dr. Ms. L. provided individual counseling for Sasha as needed. Sasha and her sisters helped each other prepare for school. She loved styling their hair. The emotional needs of the other girls were addressed in counseling too. One of Sasha's sisters became a peer mediator. Focusing on the needs of others seemed to improve her sister's confidence. This was a family of very smart girls whose home situation and behaviors collided with their learning. It was easy to see how much Ms. Curbarb meant to her students. She continued working with her class as if January's final date and surgery were not in the picture. She continued to pray every morning before class. She continued to teach her students everything she could give them before temporarily leaving. She continued to give out hugs.

Thanksgiving celebration was a highlight for Eagleville Elementary School. Thanksgiving was also a favorite event for Ms. Curbarb's students and their parents. This event brought unity to the students in classroom 302. It was a reminder of the Thanksgivings between the Pilgrims and the Indians. Cafeteria tables lined the halls on each floor of the building. Teachers, students, parents, and support staff decorated the tables with the finest Thanksgiving decorations possible. The staff, students and parents provided food and decorations. Ms. Curbarb usually cooked the turkey and some of the other customary Thanksgiving foods. The students and parents in room 302 were a family. This Thanksgiving was special because parents were able to talk with Ms. Curbarb about her illness and give well wishes. Parents also provided cell phone numbers so that she could make calls if their child's behavior was interrupting the learning process.

Following the Thanksgiving break, it was time for the Winter Break. Students in Ms. Curbarb's class, along with other students in the school, were included in many of the holiday events sponsored by Dr. Ms. L.'s partnerships. Some of Ms. Curbarb's students went on fieldtrips to have lunch with the Washington Redskins and received wish list gifts. Some students participated in the holiday fun with Howard University's Angel Tree project. Other students took a fieldtrip to the community church, New Bethel, where they were given holiday snacks, gifts for personal needs, and wish list gifts. Ms. Curbarb and Dr. Ms. L. made sure her students were included based on social emotional and economical needs.

A previous student of Ms. Curbarb's came to visit the class. It was a welcomed visit. This student shared how Ms. Curbarb had her retained in the 5th grade because she was not socially responsible and academically ready. Her behavior and failure to meet academic responsibilities was the cause of her retention. Her mom worked with Ms. Curbarb and agreed on the decision for retention. Ms. Curbarb's students could not believe that this student was "thanking" her for keeping her back in the 5th grade. At the time of this visit, this student had graduated and was employed. She talked to students about her experiences in school, repeating a grade, and moving forward. She reminded them of the awesome opportunity to be taught by Ms. Curbarb.

The next few days had peaks and challenges as Ms. Curbarb's surgical date approached. She had planned to work up to the day before her surgery, however, feelings of exhaustion and discomfort were increasing. Ms. Curbarb's birthday was quickly approaching. She showed no signs of wondering whether she would reach her birthday. Instead she came into the class and prayed each morning as usual.

The birthday board in the main office listed all of the birth dates of every child and staff in the building and it included Ms. Curbarb's birthday - January 8th. Students, staff, and parents saw the board and knew they had a few days after the winter break to plan a surprise party. Staff, friends from the school and the community, along with Ms. Curbarb's son, were also planning a party outside of the school. Ms. Curbarb's students and their parents decided to give her a surprise birthday party the first week of January 2014. This would be Ms. Curbarb's last week at school before leaving for her surgery.

Ms. Curbarb frequently taught her students to be organized and to carefully plan before doing major projects, assignments and anything that they wanted to complete successfully. Students were able to apply these principles as they planned Ms. Curbarb's surprise birthday. Coming back after the winter break was another happy milestone for students who were still uncertain about Ms. Curbarb's return to school. It was a welcome sight to see her return after the winter break. They had pushed away thoughts of her being sick with cancer. It was still unbelievable, but in the back of their minds they knew it was true, because Ms. Curbarb would not lie to them. The class continued in the denial stage of grief. Giving a surprise birthday was just a way to cope with and manage their feelings.

Her students solicited the support of parents, other students, and staff to keep Ms. Curbarb out of her room. Friday after lunch was one of her planning periods. During this period, students decorated the room with bright Happy Birthday Balloons, birthday tablecloth and rearranged the desks. The students wanted to show their love for their teacher and got their parents to support their efforts. This was one of those days when the students came together with one purpose in mind. They wanted to see the beautiful smile that they frequently get from Ms. Curbarb. They understood Ms. Curbarb would be gone for a while. They determined that on this day they would smile, they would enjoy time celebrating her, and remember her happy feelings in a place within their hearts, in order to cope with the pain of knowing that she had cancer.

Everyone had either purchased items, cooked dishes or had their parents prepare dishes that they thought Ms. Curbarb would enjoy. Some gifts were wrapped, some in gift bags, all for her to take home to remember them. It was important for the students to show her every ounce of love that they could show.

The party was a happy/sad event. Students and parents treated Ms. Curbarb like she was their mother. Ms. Curbarb had actually taught some of her student's parents and older siblings. The end of the celebration that day reminded them of Ms. Curbarb's first time disclosing on November 1, 2013 when she told the class, "I have cancer". Leaving was difficult for parents and students. Many wanted to get that last hug and were again cautious thinking that they would hurt her. Ms. Curbarb extended her arms as she had done many times before to invite them to hug her. She told them it would be all right. She also made the students promise that they would study hard and do their best on the upcoming PARCC test. Ms. Curbarb told students that, "I will fight with all my might to come back on your graduation day." Ms. Curbarb left with that beautiful smile she always seemed to have. Her faith in God was intact and would not allow her to be down. In her heart, her prayers for victory over cancer never ceased. It seemed to get stronger.

Happy Birthday to You
Happy Birthday to You
Happy Birthday Ms. Curbarb
And Many More!

CHAPTER 5

THE "BAD" KIDS IN 302 AND THE VANISHING SUBSTITUTE TEACHERS

Ms. Curbarb's medical leave occurred at a crucial time for the students in room 302. The standardized testing period was rapidly approaching. The substitute folder was full of materials to keep students working on testing strategies taught by Ms. Curbarb. Administration had not planned for a substitute teacher so they had to work swiftly to identify a substitute for Ms. Curbarb' class. Who could they find to continue what Ms. Curbarb had put in place? Who could reinforce all that Ms. Curbarb had taught? Most importantly, how would the students manage with a substitute? The students did not feel anyone could replace Ms. Curbarb. Students were now entering the anger stage of grief. Their emotions were channeled to anyone, everyone, and even to themselves. The denial stage of grief was beginning as well. The students in room 302 acted as if they were having a bad dream that could not possibly be true.

Dr. Ms. L. anticipated that the students would experience a range of emotional and behavioral reactions when they returned to school that first week after Ms. Curbarb left so special consideration had to be given to selecting a substitute. The behaviors could include changes in their appetite, sleep disturbances, withdrawal, concentration difficulties, dependency, regression, restlessness, challenging authority figures and learning difficulties. Some students might just show up to school to be with their classmates, while others simply just would not come back the first few days of Ms. Curbarb's absence.

Dr. Ms. L. noticed the students' behavior while she was on duty during breakfast times. Students got into conflicts if they felt someone looked at them in the wrong way. Some students became angry if someone sat near a friend that they normally sat with. Others played in their food or just threw a whole tray away. Some tried to go upstairs before it was time for students to go to their classroom. Some got in fights while waiting in the gym before time to go to class.

Several students in Ms. Curbarb's class seemed to be fluctuating between the first grief stage of denial and the second stage of anger. Feelings gradually moved to the second stage. The realization seemed to drop like leaves falling from trees in the fall season. Ms. Curbarb was not present for school as she had been in the past. She was not there to wave to her students as she came in the door. She did not sign in and check her mail.

Students were in a state of disbelief. Ms. Curbarb was a reliable teacher. She was almost always there so rarely did they need a substitute teacher. On a few occasions, students tolerated a substitute teacher because they knew Ms. Curbarb would address any misbehavior the next day. Misbehavior while a substitute teacher was in the classroom could mean less free time or academic work on "Fun Friday" instead of recreational games. It would also mean that Ms. Curbarb did not distribute special snacks and surprises as she often did. These were snacks and surprises that Ms. Curbarb purchased out of her own pocket. She was just that kind of teacher. Her students knew she carried each one of them home in her heart. It was unbelievable to think that she was not coming back after her birthday party. At this stage, students coped with the grief of their teacher's absence and it was progressing into anger. Some could not dismiss their misguided correlation that cancer equals death. To go on without her was overwhelming for them and it did not make sense. Sometimes they got in trouble so they could go to a different location in the building or be sent to the office or even home. Being in room 302 without Ms. Curbarb was ridiculous to them and learning seemed meaningless.

Students' behaviors seemed to suggest denial and anger. The Monday following her birthday celebration most of her students were present and on time. As they arrived, they looked into their classroom to see if somehow Ms. Curbarb had come back.

January 6, 2014 was the first day that Ms. Curbarb was not there for the students in room 302. Dr. Ms. L. was manning her usual post in the cafeteria. In their hearts they knew what she told them first on November 1, 2013 and then again on January 4, 2014 was finally coming true. They said their goodbyes at the birthday party. She shared the information about her surgery date. Despite all of the information they had been given, they expected her to be in the classroom as usual. They expected to walk in during her quiet time before class would normally begin. Some students even slipped up to her room before the designated time to see if Ms. Curbarb was there. Her door was locked. The room was dark. Students caught in the hallway were sent back to the gym.

Ms. Curbarb's absence from her classroom became the primary concern for students. "I have cancer" was at the forefront of their thoughts. The last hug she gave on her last day prior to surgery was a reality that they denied. Surely, she had to come back just one more time. However, the dark classroom was a reminder of the last Friday when she said, "I have cancer" and "I will have to have surgery and cancer treatment." Students struggled as they tried to resume a regular day.

The task of finding a substitute was not an easy one. The students in the class were separated and sent to alternate classrooms. Work packages had been provided in the substitute folder. Some students where given the chance to have extra gym time. Initially, this resolved the problem of not having their teacher; by the end of the day some students had been sent to the office, some were sent to other classrooms, several were sent to Dr. Ms. L.'s therapy room. Some students' parents were called.

Dr. Ms. L.'s room had a Child Centered Play Therapy area. Dr. Ms. L did not engage the students in dialogue, instead she allowed students to set their agenda. Students in the small girl group went immediately to the girl dolls and the doll house. They began with brushing the doll's hair and making them look nice and neat. In the past, Ms. Curbarb had combed and brushed a few of the girl's hair or sent them to the restroom to make their hair neat. With the doll house, the girls began to put things in order. In fact, they wanted to put the whole Child Centered area in order. This was their routine if they had left things out of order the day before in Ms. Curbarb's class. Their session was at the end of the school day, so they left once the Play Therapy area was neat and the bell had rung.

A small group of the boys were sent to the gym. One male student, Eddie, required a space alone. He was angry and crying. He was easily agitated if another student looked at him wrong. Anger with crying was his response to conflict. Eddie did ask if Ms. Curbarb would be in the rest of the week. Dr. Ms. L. simply shook her head no. Once he got himself together and dried his tears, Eddie went home to the support of his family.

This family - Ms. Curbarb, her students and their families - was having a challenging time with their emotions. Just as students were dealing with the cancer diagnosis, their parents were too. Some parents called to see if Ms. Curbarb was returning following her birthday party. Some parents connected Ms. Curbarb's absence with their child's sadness and contacted Dr. Ms. L. to make sure their child received counseling. Some parents also related the death of family members to the behaviors of their children. They shared information about relatives who had recently died due to cancer, but no counseling was in place following the death of their relatives. Dr. Ms. L. scheduled counseling for these students, individual and in small groups.

Allen's parent called and tearfully described the family's emotional state following the recent death of his grandfather. She said Allen would come home daily and retreat in his room to cry in private. She requested individual counseling to help Allen get through his sadness for his grandfather's death from cancer. Ms. Curbarb had already shared a list of students that she was concerned about because of drops in academic performance and Allen was one of those students. His mom expressed sad feelings because she was aware of the relationship that Allen had with Ms. Curbarb.

Allen returned to school in a very sad state. Normally a very quiet student, Allen came to an individual session overwhelmed with grief. He required a few moments of quiet followed by probing questions aimed at getting him to express his feelings. The absence of Ms. Curbarb added to his existing sadness and was more than Allen was able to manage. The sessions allowed time for him to simply cry and share. There were a few incidents of conflict with other students. This was not normal behavior for Allen at school. As the sessions progressed, Allen was asked if he wanted to write his story. Allen decided to write a book titled, *The People I Love*. Completion of this therapeutic project took a few sessions before he began to move on. He gradually moved to the bargaining stage of grief. He focused on doing his work, not giving the substitute teachers any difficulty, and the stopping of crying by the end of each day. He felt he could make things better for Ms. Curbarb if his behavior improved.

Dr. Ms. L. searched for books about teachers who experienced cancer during the school year. There were books like *Mom Has Cancer* by Marta Fabrega and *When Your Mom Has Cancer* by Maryann Makeckau.

Since Ms. Curbarb was a second mother figure to her students, the books had some similarities' to her situation, but not enough. Additional research revealed articles about teachers experiencing cancer. Their stories were mostly about how they dealt with their students once they returned to school and some of the things that happened while they were out. The stories they disclosed, in many cases, were different from Ms. Curbarb's story. Ms. Curbarb shared her diagnosis with her students following the confirmation of her final diagnosis and the knowledge that she would need immediate surgery. Her students had to deal with her being "here today" and the potential for being "gone tomorrow". She could not tell them how long she would be out, but the one thing she was sure of and had faith in, was that she would return for their graduation. This was her promise to her students.

There ended up being at least six substitute teachers while Ms. Curbarb was out. Some substitutes left after one or two days, some for a week, and they did not sign up for return assignments. One substitute teacher left the classroom and did not return to the school for assignments in other classes either. Administration had to intervene because some substitutes did not give much warning about not returning. Gym and music time were increased. Administration was only able to manage students' behaviors for limited times due to other responsibilities in the school. To add to the challenges, students did not seem ready for a full day of learning.

Dr. Ms. L. and Ms. Speeds, the school psychologist, conducted group sessions like "Managing Emotions" where students shared diverse emotions and incidents related to those emotions. They also shared their emotions regarding Ms. Curbarb's illness. Ms. Curbarb's 5th grade class was a very cohesive group. During one of Dr. Ms. L's sessions she asked students to write a letter of encouragement to one of their classmates. Dr. Ms. L. matched students that did not normally "hangout" together, and students that had previous conflicts with each other. Initially, the students did not like the idea, but they cooperated. Students were asked to make sure their letter was a one of encouragement. The cohesiveness of this group of students was evident as they read their letters out loud to the person that they were assigned to write about. Several of the students relished what had been written about them and wanted to keep the letters. The student group evolved from being in conflict and full of anger to a loving and caring group who shared the pain of what was going on with their teacher. During another session with the students, Dr. Ms. L. had a "talk out" session. The only rule was to talk one at a time so that they could be clearly heard. Students were angry because they were called a "bad" class because of repeated episodes of misbehavior and because they had so many different substitute teachers. Dr. Ms. L. explained to them that some of their behavior had to do with the trauma of what was happening with their teacher and not knowing when or if she would be back. Trauma had also stemmed from other events in their lives. The students collectively agreed. They said that administration did not understand them. Dr. Ms. L. offered the opportunity for the principal to come to their class to listen to their concerns. The students were given the freedom to express themselves, with respect, in front of the principal. The principal was asked to acknowledge and respect the student's feelings by simply listening and not saying a word. The students informed the principal that they did not like the adjectives used to describe their class. They talked about the lack of commitment from some of the substitute teachers. One substitute was blind and they really did not understand how he could help them. Yet they said he was somewhat caring. They said no one seemed to understand what they were going through. There were a few times when they felt that others "temporarily" understood them. They said no one cared about them like Ms. Curbarb did. At the end of the session, the classroom was silent. The principal thanked the students and left the room with tears in her eyes. Her silence meant more than anything she could say.

Dr. Ms. L. provided Ms. Curbarb with frequent updates about her students. She also inquired about her progress on some of her good days. In return, she provided updates of Ms. Curbarb's progress to the students. Ms. Curbarb also sent her regards to the students through Dr. Ms. L.

Ms. Curbarb was concerned about her student's progress and their readiness for testing. She and Dr. Ms. L. decided to do a class via Skype on a day when Ms. Curbarb felt up to it. The students had great anticipation about that plan. On the selected day, all students were present at school. Efforts to connect the classroom to Skype failed. Dr. Ms. L. decided to use her cell phone to make sure that the class was able to at least hear Ms. Curbarb and interact with her verbally. Dr. Ms. L. was determined to not disappoint the students, who needed a little bit of hope before the PARCC test. She pulled out her little red cellphone. Students were asked to be completely quiet except when they were reading or responding to Ms. Curbarb. They were informed that she would be asking questions and listening to them read and respond. Students were 100% cooperative that day. Every student read a portion of the story to her. They answered vocabulary questions. They stated the main ideas in the story and identified it with supporting information. Ms. Curbarb was able to tell that students could demonstrate some of the lessons she taught. Students were able to gain hope that Ms. Curbarb could still teach them.

Dr. Ms. L. selected a story from the book, *Everyday Heroes* by Beth Johnson. Stories in this book are about children of various ages and cultures living in stressful situations. The stories told about how they were able to learn from mistakes, challenges, behavior crisis and turn their lives around for a positive outlook. Stories in the book were similar to some of the life hurdles experienced by students in room 302.

The cooperation students gave at that time seemed to put them in the bargaining stage of their grief. They all seemed to realize how much they had accomplished in room 302. They all seemed to understand the correlation of behavior and achievement. If only Ms. Curbarb came back, then they could show her how involved they were with learning. If only Ms. Curbarb came back, they would be the best students she would ever have.

CHAPTER 6

WE ARE STILL PRAYING FOR YOU

After the phone call with Ms. Curbarb, students returned to a classroom without their dear teacher. They remembered the promises that they made to her. The substitute teachers were not Ms. Curbarb, but at least they had become familiar to the class. The students did the work Ms. Curbarb had left for them. It seemed liked they were content with having papers that Ms. Curbarb had touched. This would offer some comfort for her not actually being with them.

During one of the group sessions with the students, Dr. Ms. L. and Ms. Speeds picked a day to have the students write encouraging notes to Ms. Curbarb while she was receiving cancer treatment . Students wrote letters and decorated cards with butterflies and get-well teddy bears. Their writing contained many grammatical errors, however, the feelings they had for Ms. Curbarb were flawless. A sampling of what students wrote on the cards follows: (Content of the cards are exactly as student wrote them.)

Dear Ms. Curbarb,

I love you so much. Ms. Curbarb, I hope to see you soon. Do you know I love you soooo much? I just want to hug you right now.

I know I am not a perfect student, but I know that I can do my best. Ms. Curbarb this is the most helpful week for me. I hope the best for you.

Student

When things are tough

Our love too

Sasha

I love you; you will be healed and will back soon. You are the Shining Star. You are the best. I love you

Steven

Ms. Curbarb,

I hope you feel better and I want to see you come back at our graduation.

Yoruba

Ms. Curbarb,

I know you had trust in us to do better and where trying for you and us too.

I hope you feel better also. I have not been laughing too much.

Also, I got Advance in my reading. I had problems in math but I am trying. DON'T FORGET YOUR FAMILY.

FAVORITE
TEACHER

Dear Ms. Curbarb,

I come to you first to thank God for you being my teacher. When you gave us the news about your health, it hurt me so bad because I don't want you to be sick. I want you to know I love you and I will pray every night that God watch over your health. I know our God will love you.

Allen

Dear Ms. Curbarb,

May God heal you with his mighty powers and your mind be at ease. Please, I love you with all my heart. Please do not let your illness drift us apart.

One of you true loves,
Mavis

Hi Ms. Curbarb,

How are you doing? I've been taking notes in classes. We're reading dramas like Shakespeare. I think I got my retelling better. The basketball team beat a team called Langton by 20. The score was 28 to 8. Math is getting a little harder.

Sincerely,
Troy

Dear Ms. Curbarb,

I love you so much. Ms. Curbarb, I hope to see you soon. Do you know I love you so much? I just want to hug you right now! How are you doing? I'm working hard just as if you were here. I wish I can see you lifting my soul and spirits. I am crying as I write this because I love you. I hope to see you teach again and I promise I will do better. I will pray at least once a day. I will study my words and also, I will get even better at division. I will be respectful to all teachers. God will heal you and make sure you get better. He will also watch over you and make sure nothing happens to you. If you serve God, God will serve you. I will not get any attitudes with my substitute teachers. I will tell you when I accomplish anything, even if it is a little. I apologized for all the things I did wrong.

Very Strong Love,
Diamond

Best Teacher in the Whole Wide World. I love you this much: XOXO XOXO XOXO XOXO XOXO XOXO XOXO XOXO XOXO.

You did so much for me and my classmates. I have been praying for you.

I LOVE
YOU

Ms. Curbarb,

I hope you get better and get to see us a lot. I also hope that you will still be our fifth-grade teacher. I love you so much and I just feel hurt. I don't want you to die because I am going to be heart broken. I wish you come to school every day. I just love you so much and everyone in my house going to be heart broken. I love you so much. You are the best teacher and only teacher I will love always and forever. I will miss you forever and really wish you can stay our teacher. I always and forever love you.

Love your student
Katy

MS. CURBARB
WE LOVE YOU
WE MISS YOU
WE ARE PRAYING
FOR YOU.

CHAPTER 7

GRADUATION

Students received encouragement from Ms. Curbarb by telephone just before the PARCC testing. Additionally, Dr. Ms. L. continued to provide them with updates of her treatment progress. The school year was coming to an end for Ms. Curbarb's 5th grade students. Letters with graduation requirements, fees, and dress codes were sent home with students. Still there was no news about Ms. Curbarb's return. Since students had not received news that Ms. Curbarb had died, their anxieties switched to marching rehearsals, chorus practice, graduation speeches and planning for after graduation parties. Dr. Ms. L. assumed the responsibilities of putting the graduation program together while Ms. Curbarb advised from home. Their goal was to make sure everything was perfect for this 5th grade class.

After the PARCC testing, students began the end of the year activities including a full day of recreational activity that taught sportsmanship, team building, and included games in and outdoors. After students ate regular healthy lunches, they got a chance to buy food similar to carnival food. Ms. Curbarb traditionally had a cookout for her 5th grade students. Since she would not be sponsoring it this year, the 5th graders went on a skating trip accompanied by other staff members that usually supported the graduation activities. The skating trip was a high energy activity that helped students reduce their anxieties about graduation. The event also seemed to take the student's mind off Ms. Curbarb's situation. Ms. Curbarb's students seemed to be riding an emotional roller coaster during this time. Their behavior caused some to be excluded from some parts of the activity. Practice for the graduation focused more on behavior management than actual practice. At one point the music teacher threatened to end rehearsal unless he had full cooperation. Ms. Curbarb's students wanted graduation, but they wanted it with her present. Several staff members stepped in to make sure the graduation event was like she would have it to be. They supplied items such as the cake, cups, plates and other things needed for the reception. Ms. Curbarb and Dr. Ms. L. worked together to make sure every student had the clothes they needed for graduation. Additionally, Dr. Ms. L. and other staff members paid the graduation fees for some students who needed the support.

Meanwhile from home, Ms. Curbarb was having some good days; she was able to direct Dr. Ms. L. and others to work with identified students to give graduation speeches and she also offered assistance with the graduation program design.

By graduation time, Ms. Curbarb had lost most of her hair from the cancer treatment. She had to wear a mask whenever out in public to avoid contracting germs that would complicate her condition. She was gaining strength daily but not enough to come to the school. However, as graduation time grew near, Ms. Curbarb felt she could possibly attend graduation. She did not want to fully commit to being involved with the graduation ceremony because of the instability of her condition from day to day.

After some time, Ms. Curbarb finally decided that she wanted to attend the graduation ceremony. Her presence would be a surprise for the students, parents and staff. Kirk, her son, agreed to take her to the graduation and seat her before others could crowd around her. Crowds were avoided because of the need to avoid germ exposure.

On the day of graduation, Ms. Curbarb was dressed in her white suit and shoes just like she had done many times before. She decided not to cover her bald head. She sat on the left side of the event room which placed her almost to the back of her students. She watched as they marched in perfectly synchronized with the music. She watched as they received various awards which she selected for her students. She also listened to and watched them sing their graduation song, Hezekiah Walker's "I Need You to Survive":

> I need you, you need me.
> We're all a part of God's body.
> Stand with me, agree with me.
> We're all a part of God's body.
> It is his will, that every need be supplied.
> You are important to me; I need you to survive.
> You are important to me; I need you to survive.
> I pray for you; you pray for me.
> I love you; I need you to survive.
> I won't harm you with words from my mouth.
> I love you; I need you to survive.
> It is his will, that every need be supplied.
> You are important to me; I need you to survive.

It was at this point that the final stages of grief - depression and acceptance - were observed. The students sang the song from the depths of their hearts. They did not see Ms. Curbarb. Her absence seemed to cause sadness and forced them to consider the loss of their teacher's presence this last year of elementary school. As depression threatened to loom over the graduation events, Ms. Curbarb students seemed to accept that they would not see her again.

The ceremony included time for students to give portfolios and flowers to the people that had helped them reach the milestone of graduation from the 5th grade . Afterwards it was the time for the 5th grade teachers to read the names of their students and present them with their promotion certificates. Ms. Curbarb's students were asked to stand. The administrator, with tears flooding her face, was aware that Ms. Curbarb was in the room and asked her to come forth to award her students. It was indeed a moment for tears and cheers by everyone present for the event.

Ms. Curbarb, a short lady in stature, walked proudly to the microphone with that smile that her students were used to seeing. Without a word, her stance said, *"I promised that I would come back for your graduation."* Students maintained their composure and the uniformity that they had practiced. With smiles and tears, they each accepted the promotional certificates and gave flowers to Ms. Curbarb. Finally, they were all granted a chance to hug Ms. Curbarb one more time.

Ms. Curbarb's recovery seemed to improve after she kept her promise to her students. According to her, keeping her promise was the greatest accomplishment through her faith journey against cancer.

A teacher knows how to steer a child towards learning even
when they don't want to go.

A teacher knows how to be mother in the classroom and still
send a child home to their mom.

A teacher knows how to live by example without forcing
her belief on every student.

A teacher knows how to fill the gaps in a child's emotion with
love and not take over their parent's position.

A teacher with faith knows that by praying and believing God
will answer.

A teacher knows how to educate a child by giving them their
needed portions of learning and not wasting time with resistance.

A teacher knows how to make a lifelong impact without forcing
her/his will on a student.

A teacher knows how to share her wisdom and keep enough for
the next group of students.

A school social worker knows how to identify the "person in
situation" without taking away the strength and identity.

A school social worker knows how to build collaboration
between teacher, student, parent, and all other stakeholders.

The school social worker knows how invite all participants into
the solution.

The school social worker knows that families are created in
diverse places.

DR. CYNTHIA LOCKE HENDERSON

ABOUT THE AUTHOR

Dr. Cynthia Henderson is a social worker who has worked in the family, medical, death and dying and K-12 school settings. She has served as a school social worker for 26 years. In her profession, she has maintained a desire to help people improve their lives.

Dr. Henderson's undergraduate studies were completed at Fayetteville State University, master's studies in Social Work at Howard University, and doctoral studies at Howard University and the International Graduate Center.

Dr. Henderson is a gifted writer, presenter, and poetess. She has completed a book of original rhyming poetry titled "Standing in The Midst of Trying Circumstance". Additionally, she has written several single poems targeted for special populations and events. One of her favorite poems is "The Person Living Within". She has also written "Love Letter from God" that has been instrumental in helping many find their deliverance in God during difficult times. Her book, "Healing Until I Am Healed" was published in November 2015. She has begun a series of children therapeutic books to address social-emotional concerns. "Touching the Lives of Others" and a prayer journal are currently being edited for publication.

Dr. Henderson has served for several years as the writer of monthly letters of encouragement that were sent to the ladies on her church's listserv and friends. She not only writes for herself; she inspires students to write. A highlight of her work with challenging students was the opportunity to get General Education and Special Education students to love writing. Writing allowed the students to turn their scars of abuse, neglect, abandonment, and more into stories. This project has been replicated over 12 years by other Writing Project Teachers.

Her writing has yielded thousands of dollars in grants to improve resources for teachers who teach low-income students in the urban setting.

Dr. Henderson was accepted in the District of Columbia Area Writing Project (DCAWP) in 1995 when she requested an opportunity to learn what teachers needed from students to ensure their academic success. In turn, she could incorporate the concerns of teachers in her intervention with students. She believed that she could provide a link between students and teachers to yield a successful learning partnership. Dr. Henderson was the first social worker to become a Teacher Consultant for the National Writing Project and in the local District of Columbia Area Writing Project. As a Teacher Consultant, she has presented at conferences throughout the United States and abroad - Boudreaux, France, Ulrich the Netherland, St. Kitts, and Israel. She was selected to serve as the Project Outreach Coordinator assisting with the writing of a three-year grant project to study the impact of the Writing Project for teachers in a low-income area. Added to her success, she was highly influential in creating The New Teacher's Network, to encourage teachers to remain in the profession of teaching and supporting them through the concept of Teachers on Call (TOC). This venture led to the creation of a New Teachers Initiative with the National Writing Project.

As a clinical social worker, she was selected as the Social Worker of the Year in 1995 and 2007 for the NASW District of Columbia Chapter. Social workers are usually awarded this position only once. Dr. Henderson is also featured in the "200 Years of Public Education in the Nation's Capital 1804-2014" and was selected as the 2019 Lifetime Social Worker of the Year.

Serving a second term on the Washington Teacher Union Executive Board, Dr. Henderson advocates for social workers and teachers in the District of Columbia Public Schools. She continues to seek opportunities to create lifelong learning opportunities between teachers, students, and parents.

Dr. Henderson is the proud mother of four adult children and six grand-children; among them are two sets of twin girls. She attends New Vision Church where she is a member of the Women's Ministry, Presentations Ministry, and a member of the Fabulous Seasoned Community group. Her love for the Lord stems from going to church with her mom and watching God prove himself to her family multiple times. She accredits her gift and life to Christ. She's often said, "I am because God is and because God has ordered the steps in my life." Her current life theme is We Walk Together (WWT).